# The McGraw-Hill Guide to Presentation Graphics

**David S. Birdsell**
*School of Public Affairs*
*Baruch College, CUNY*

**Boston Burr Ridge, IL Dubuque, IA Madison, WI New York San Francisco St. Louis**
**Bangkok Bogotá Caracas Lisbon London Madrid**
**Mexico City Milan New Delhi Seoul Singapore Sydney Taipei Toronto**

***WCB/McGraw-Hill***

*A Division of The* ***McGraw·Hill*** *Companies*

The McGraw-Hill Guide to Presentation Graphics



1 2 3 4 5 6 7 8 9 0 BKM/BKM 9 0 9 8

ISBN 0-07-007019-9

www.mhhe.com

# Table of Contents

## What Are Presentation Graphics?

At the simplest level, presentation graphics (PG) are visual materials designed to supplement an oral presentation. They can consist of verbal outlines, graphs, pictures, even videos – anything designed to support what a speaker says, to make it more memorable, more exciting, or easier to understand.

In the 1990s, the term most often refers specifically to visual materials produced on a computer. Powerful programs such as Adobe Persuasion™, Corel Presentations™, Gold Disk Astound™, Lotus Freelance Graphics™, and Microsoft PowerPoint™, allow speakers to incorporate attractive, audience-specific backgrounds, sophisticated graphs, text animations, and even videoclips into a single, integrated presentation design. You don't have to be a graphic artist to use these programs. Their forgiving, graphical user interfaces (GUIs) and online help allow almost anyone who knows his or her way around a contemporary word processor to develop sophisticated presentations.

But there's a catch. To get the most out of your presentation package, you need to know *when* to use its tools, and *why*. You need to know *how* some basic concepts can speed you through the process of designing and delivering presentations. You also need to know about some of the major *pitfalls* of computer-assisted presentation and how to avoid them. Finally, you need to know where to find *resources* for additional assistance with the programs themselves, and to achieve a richer understanding of elements such as graphs, animations, etc.

## How to Use this Booklet

This is a guide to certain basic concepts and practices in PG; it is *not* a software manual. You'll read a lot here about what to embrace and what to avoid, but you won't learn how to achieve a particular effect in a given program. For that level of detail, you should consult the documentation that shipped with your software. You can, however, use the practices described here to decide what you need to learn next, and how to incorporate that information into your presentation design.

Most importantly, this booklet is about *public speaking*. PG software can be used to design a multitude of products, such as kiosk-based presentations, computer-based training programs, and merchandising booklets. Useful applications all, they have very little to do with the practices that work best for someone delivering an oral presentation. While pointing out some of the automated capabilities of presentation packages, we will keep our focus tightly trained on speaking, an activity that demands that the presenter always be in control of his or her tools.

We'll start with a section describing what PG can – and cannot – do for your speeches. We will then move into a discussion of the basic concepts and processes that drive the most popular software packages. Just as important as the list of "to-dos," we will cover a brief list of common mistakes so that you won't have to make them in front of an audience yourself. Finally, we'll look at how you can use some of the more advanced capabilities of these programs, and where to find more information about various topics introduced here.

## What Presentation Graphics Can Do for You

The benefits of PG fall into three basic categories: making it easier for the audience to follow and remember your presentation; illustrating complex concepts with images; and providing you with a aids for organization and pacing. Let's look at each benefit individually.

### Navigation and Recall

Speakers ask a lot of their audiences. You want people to follow an often complex line of reasoning, or to remember involved procedures, or keep several sets of numbers in their heads. Imagine that you were trying to convince people of the marketing potential of the World Wide Web. Early in your presentation, you'll probably want to define the Web so that your audience knows what you're talking about. You can do that in words alone, but it would more memorable to provide a slide like the following:

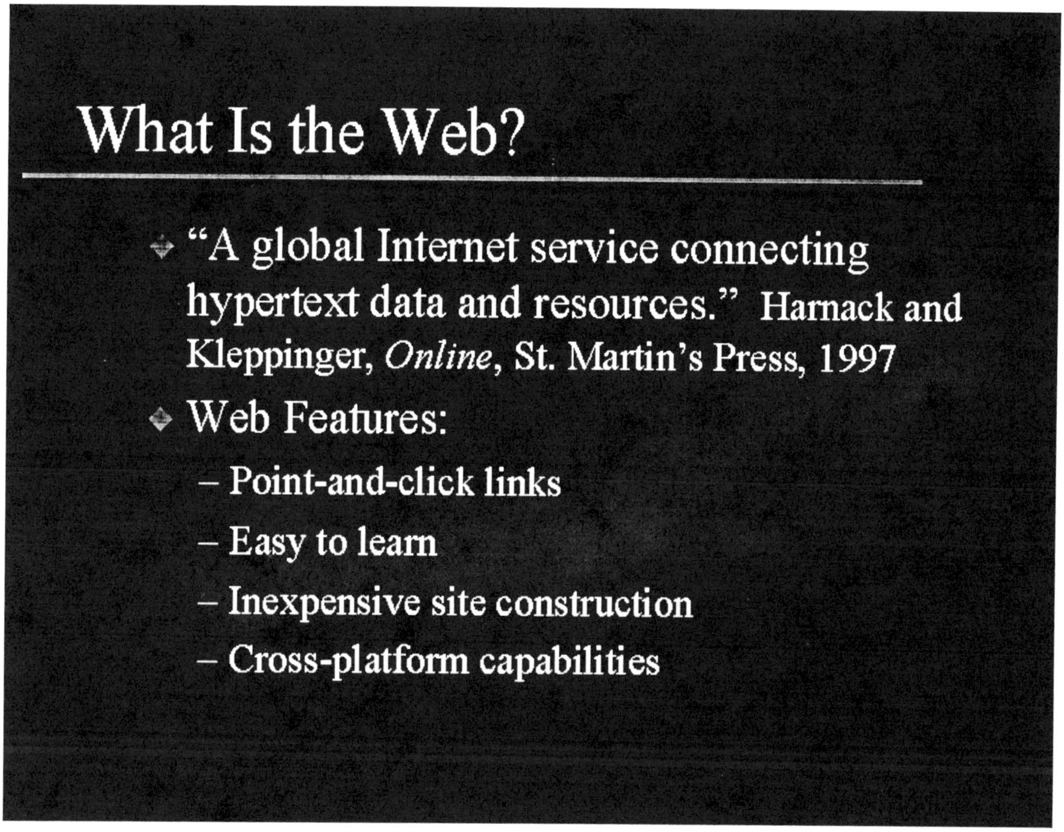


Using a text slide such as this allows your audience to see what you're saying, fixing the point more firmly in their minds. It also helps to identify how you're splitting up the topic. In this case, an audience can clearly see what features are central, and which are supporting portions of the narrative.

Note that with this slide and in fact, most slides in this booklet, the basic background remains the same. The specific content and design of each slide may change, but each is recognizable as a member of a consistent design family. This basic background is called a "template." A properly chosen template lends visual coherence to your presentation. Most PG packages give you many template options, and some allow you to create templates of your own. More than visually appealing, however, the template serves a cognitive function as well. By putting textual and graphical materials in the same places relative to titles, page numbers, and other items, the template makes it easier for the audience to focus on content. This is one of the most powerful tools that PG packages offer in terms of making presentations more navigable and memorable.

**Illustrative Images**

PG packages allow the incorporation of many types of images. This is very handy for the speaker who needs to discuss statistical relationships, explain the physical layout of a space, or refer to specific visual elements. In the following illustration, a complex set of relationships among sub-groups of the Internet user population is made more readily understandable by incorporating the figures on a graph. A speaker could, of course, simply repeat the figures for the audience, but

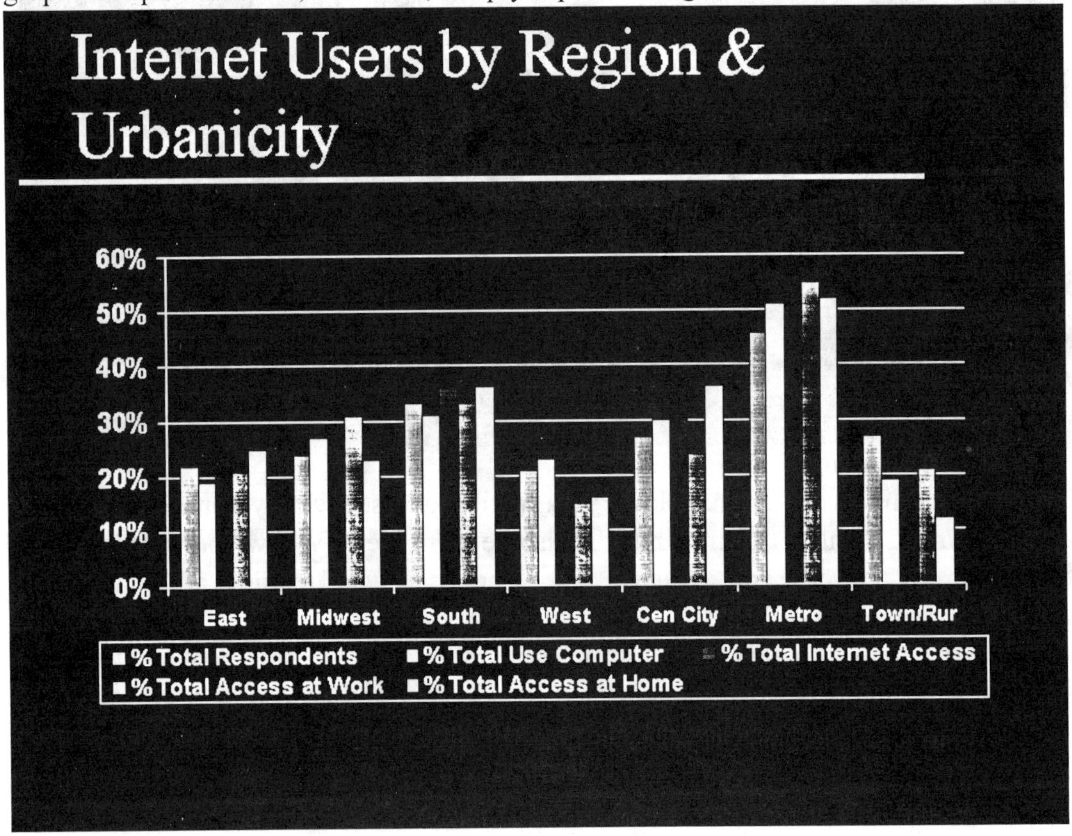


Data from Baruch Harris Survey Unit, April 1997

there are several disadvantages to that approach. First, it requires the speaker to go over a lot of information that won't figure directly in his or her conclusions. Second, it asks the audience to keep several levels of statistics in mind at the same time. That is, in order to make sense of these data, the audience will have to remember what percentage of the general population lives in metro areas in order to assess the different percentages of computer users and Internet users resident in metro areas.

The graph puts all the data in one place, allowing the audience to follow along as a speaker spends his or her time drawing attention to the most important issues. No one in the audience has to work overtime to remember a lot of numbers (which may not be important anyway), but they are given powerful tools to help them discern the relationships among numbers (almost always the point of presenting information of this sort).

In addition to graphs, speakers can provide photographic images, room layouts, mechanical drawings, and other illustrations of concepts or objects that are difficult to describe by words alone. If you have any doubts about how useful this can be, try an experiment. Describe to a friend the layout of furniture in your bedroom. Time yourself to see how long it takes you. Then give your friend a test to see what he or she remembered. Next, to another friend, describe the same room with the aid of a carefully prepared diagram showing the arrangement of furniture. You can repeat the test as many times as you want, and there will of course be differences in your friends' responses, no matter how you describe the room. But in general, you'll find that you save time in the explanation and your audience will remember more when the layout is illustrated.

**Tools for Organization and Delivery**

Many speakers, particularly beginning speakers, are bedeviled by reliance on manuscripts. For most speeches, you should strive to deliver from a topical outline rather than a prepared manuscript. Outlines give you all of the benefits of careful preparation with none of the rigidity of a complete text.

The text portion of a PG program can help you make the appropriate adjustments in several ways. First, the built-in outlining functions encourage you to think through your overheads as part and parcel of the substance of the presentation reflected in your notes. The audience sees what you see as they hear what you have prepared, giving them a second means of access into your structure.

Second, your program will give you at least three means of supplementing your basic outline. Speaker's notes provide a visual thumbnail of each slide and an area where you can write in additional information such as source materials, or data that you don't want to display on the screen. Outline views (typically available from either a "View" or a "Print" menu) let you see a running outline of the presentation from beginning to end. This makes it easy to see how your presentation hangs together between screens. The clean, text-only format of the outline view also helps you to focus on your argument rather than on the graphic arrangement of the presentation. You can also assemble handouts, which provide you with prefabricated forms for distributing materials to members of the audience. These will typically represent exactly what is on a display slide, but most programs allow you to provide running annotation in the form of page headers or footers.

Third, your PG package will help you edit your work without having to recreate whole sequences of the presentation. "Slide Sorter" views display all of the slides on a single page. If you want to change the order in which the slides are presented, you can simply drag a slide to a new location using your mouse.

The importance of editing flexibility is hard to overstate. Even the most experienced speakers need to edit their first attempts at a presentation. Any tool that makes the editing process easier makes it more likely that the editing will actually take place in a thoughtful, timely fashion. Make sure to take advantage of these high-tech tools for achieving very traditional goals.

When it comes time to deliver your presentation, the slideshow can help you. The slides serve as a set of notes in and of themselves. You can use the slides to time yourself and get a fairly accurate idea of how long it takes you to discuss the issues presented on each one. Knowing that you have five slides to go can help prevent you from spending too much time on the early materials. As noted above, the slides can also save time by making difficult concepts easier for the audience to understand. This allows you to shift away from the unrewarding task of merely conveying information in favor of making the broader points that drive your speech.

## What Presentation Graphics *Cannot* Do

You'll notice that there is no reference here to creating an "impression." Impressions are important in public speaking, but no single tool can make a good impression, even a powerful, multimedia presentation package. A poorly conceived PG show can actually detract from your presentation. In particular, do not look to your PG package to:

- "Automatically" generate materials appropriate to your topic and audience. The software will help you edit and encourage you to organize, but you have to make the basic decisions. Some PG packages do ship with prepared speech types, with such labels as "sales," "bad news," or "persuasion." While you might find some of these prepared outlines useful, do not make the mistake of relying on them. Speaking is about adapting to a situation, and these prefabricated outlines are, by definition, generic. They may also conflict with some specific recommendations that your instructor has made throughout the semester. Use whatever tools you find helpful, but do not operate on the assumption that the most general approaches are well-suited to your needs.

- Allow you to bypass other elements of speech preparation. PG software cannot do your research, analyze your audience, identify supporting materials, or practice your presentation. These speech basics remain your responsibility.

Now that you have a basic understanding of what presentation packages do and do not do, we can move on to the concepts and practices that drive the creation of successful presentations.

## Basic Concepts

Before you do anything else with PG software, you need to put the package in its proper place. Always remember that the slideshow is a tool, not the speech itself. Your audience has come to hear *you*, not to see a show. If the graphics package comes between you and the audience in any way, it is likely to become more of a hindrance than an asset. Your goal as both designer and presenter should be to *support the presentation*, not to supplant that presentation with a sideshow that detracts from your speech.

Unfortunately, it's not hard to fall into the distraction trap. For example, many contemporary PG packages provide sophisticated tools for integrating multimedia elements. They make it easy to incorporate sound effects, videoclips, and other multimedia elements. Used judiciously, they can greatly enhance a presentation, but used carelessly, they get in the way. Some presenters play background music during portions of their presentations, impeding the natural give-and-take between speaker and audience. Others try to include animated or motion video elements on every slide, breaking up the flow of the presentation, in essence competing with the speaker. Finally, many presenters make the mistake of standing well off to the side during a presentation, allowing their graphics to occupy center stage. The presenter largely disappears while the slideshow becomes the "messenger."

In this section, we will discuss a five-step system to ensure that the PG package supports your presentation. This is not a section on how to put a speech together – your main text covers that. We will start from the point at which you have analyzed your audience, delineated your topic, identified supporting materials, and organized the basic presentation. Our discussion will focus on the PG component per se.

## Using the P-E-T-A-L System

In conceptualizing every presentation, you will have to develop *Pertinent* materials, choose an *Engaging* format, present your materials in a *Timely* manner, satisfy yourself that they are *Appropriate* to the audience, and ensure that everything is *Legible*. We will deal with each of these requirements below.

### Pertinent

Everything in your presentation should be pertinent to your topic. That means the basic template design, any special features, the words on a text slide, and the graphs you choose to create. Never include an element simply for effect; it will detract attention from your central purpose if it is not tightly tied into the basic message you want to convey to your audience.

Many presenters make this mistake with clip art, introducing random images simply because they're available on the computer's hard drive. We'll look more closely at the risks and benefits of clip art below. For now, it's enough to know that a picture, no matter how pretty, should go into your presentation only if it makes a point that is central to your presentation in a more efficient fashion than it could be made otherwise.

### Engaging

Your slideshow will be most engaging if it incorporates judicious use of color, a consistent, uncluttered design format, and relatively limited text. The default colors built into most PG templates have been selected to promote clarity and engagement both; it's best to use them unless you have a specific reason for choosing another color. One such reason might be the characteristics of the display device you use for the presentation. Some monitors and/or projectors deal differently with different colors, making a red hard to distinguish from a violet, or a blue from a green. Make sure that the default colors you see in the design window actually look like the same colors on the equipment you will use to reach your audience.

Assuming that you start with a well-designed template, clutter comes principally from trying to crowd too many elements onto the screen and using overly complicated or inconsistent graphic conventions. Let's start with the graphic conventions. Most templates that you choose will enforce a degree of uniformity in bulleting, numbering, titling, etc. If the major headings are indicated by a diamond on page one, they should be indicated by a diamond on page two. If sub-heads are indicated by a dot on page one, they should be indicated by a dot on page two, and so on.

Some presentation designers want to customize their presentations by choosing their own bullets. That's fine – actually a good move – *if* the elements are a) few in number, and b) consistently applied. Few audience members will remember a complex, multi-level bulleting system, no matter how unusual the graphics. Remember that when you design graphic elements, a meaning that is perfectly plain to you may not be plain at all to your audience. Keeping it simple, indicating order and not substance, improves your chances of making visual sense to your audience.

Sticking with a manageable set of screen elements is a matter of personal discipline and case-by-case judgment, but some general rules do apply. First, never put so much text on a slide that an audience is encouraged to read the slide and stop listening to you. The text should be short and substantive, guiding the discussion and indicating its direction, but never becoming the discussion itself.

Second, when using large graphic elements such as graphs or pictures, try not to have more than a single element on a slide (an exception would be side-by-side comparisons of two pieces of art, or other circumstances where the simultaneous presentation of images is central to the purpose of the speech). They can be accompanied by text – most presentation packages have slide templates for a graph or an image flanked by bullets – but typically not other featured graphic elements.

Third, never "decorate" your slides. Materials intended to make light, seasonal references may seem amusing but they can be deeply confusing to an audience trying to understand a graph. Imagine someone presenting a corporate report who festoons a performance graph with holiday ribbons (a trick seen all too often). The ribbons themselves may be mistaken for data points on the graph; the clutter will have overtaken the substance, turning the "decor" into a potentially disastrous mistake.

**Timely**

Slides should be placed where they are needed in the presentation, not before, and not after their oral complement has been delivered. In order to assure timeliness, it is important to stick to the outline you've prepared. Jumping around in the presentation becomes evident to the audience in a slideshow format, even in cases where they might not have noticed had the speech been given orally, without visual support.

PG software includes tools to enhance timeliness within the frame. Slide "builds" allow you to bring each heading in a text slide onto the screen in sequence. "Dimming" or "graying" functions turn text you've covered into a lighter shade or a different color, making your focus plain to the audience. Use these tools to help audiences stay on track, improving the match between word and image in your presentations.

**Appropriate**

The graphic support you choose must be appropriate to your audience, your topic, and your situation. Remember that graphic design is in enormous flux today. Younger audiences, raised on *Spin* and *Vibe* may tolerate a good deal more graphic experimentation than older, more staid audiences. Choose your template designs and your featured graphic elements accordingly.

Topics may not seem at first glance to require particular treatments, and while there are indeed many ways to approach any given issue, some graphical environments are distinctly inappropriate for certain topics. You would not, for example, want to choose a template featuring balloons and confetti for a speech arguing that social sororities and fraternities offer students important educational opportunities. You would not want to choose a bright, starry motif for a presentation about starvation in Sub-Saharan Africa. Even a more subtle disjunction between message and medium can create misunderstanding in your audience.

Situation, in this case, refers to the specific circumstances of your presentation. Take account of the presentation equipment you'll be using. Will it be a slide projector? An overhead projector? A fully computerized LCD projector? Will you be able to display colors? Will you be able to use slide build features? These are important questions that need to be taken into account in the basic design process.

**Legible**

No presentation, no matter how well conceived, can succeed if your audience cannot see what you've designed. Start where we left off in the last section, with the presentation environment. If you cannot use a computer, but must print out your slides to sheets of acetate, make sure that the printer you use can replicate the screen colors faithfully. If not, change the colors to what looks good on the output side; that's what your audience will see. By the same token, if you use black and white output for a design that began as a color design, make sure that the screen elements can still be distinguished from one another. Two clearly distinct shades of red may look much the same in black and white; don't make the mistake of assuming that you can judge the black and white appearance solely on the basis of apparent color discrepancies.

Font sizes, which we will cover in more depth a little later, should be big enough to be seen by everyone in the room. A corollary to this rule is that you should never sacrifice legibility to get more material onto the screen. If you must use more text than you can fit onto the screen, use a second screen; don't shrink the fonts to the point where you lose people in the back rows.

For all legibility issues, the key is testing in the room. Screen elements that appear perfectly legible in one format may be entirely obscure in another. Some presenters rely on delicate screen elements only to find out that the rooms in which they have been scheduled to present have too much natural light for the smaller devices to show up at all! Checking your site and your materials in advance – ideally, before designing the presentation – will help you avoid this problem.

## Basic Processes: Construction

We're now ready to take a look at some basic considerations in actually designing your presentation. You will find that your PG package is a rich environment that affords you a great deal of flexibility. Most PG software adapts very well to different levels of expertise. The point-and-click design of the templates allows a beginner to get up and running very quickly, while the more advanced drawing and custom templating features support expert users. We'll stick to some basic, very nearly universal concepts here: the slide metaphor, use of templates, and the various views of your work that most packages make available. We'll then take a quick look at what works best with text slides, and how to begin to assemble your graphic elements.

**The Slide Metaphor**

We have consistently referred to "slides," and "slideshows" in discussions of presentation design in this booklet. In fact, unless you use a service bureau or have access to a slide printer yourself, you won't be using slides per se. The slide is a metaphor for how the presentation looks, and how it is organized. All of the packages mentioned on the first page (and several others as well) support the slide metaphor.

In a computer PG package, the slide is the basic element of each design. There are many types of slides and a plethora of templates. Some slides are reserved for titles, others for bullets, others for graphs, and still others for combinations of text and graphic material. The slide provides the designer with a frame in which to arrange the elements of a subsection of a speech. Typically, each slide indicates a major subdivision, though in a lengthy talk of twenty minutes or more, each slide may represent a relatively small portion of the overall presentation.

It is very important to remember that each slide is a *piece* of the presentation, not the whole thing. Many mistakes are made by designers who try to put too much information onto one slide, obscuring important points amid a welter of smaller issues. It is equally important to remember that no slide (unless there's only one!) stands on its own. It must function as part of an integrated presentation design that itself serves the concept behind a public speech.

In addition to serving as the basis for design, the slide is also the basis for presentation. When you assemble your slides, think about how you will relate to the material your audience can see. Strive for balance from slide to slide, allocating roughly equivalent content to each so that the presentation seems to move forward in predictable segments. Remember that the slide has to remain visible for a long enough period of time to allow the audience to absorb its content. Flashing graphs in front of confused listeners serves no one; if an idea is important enough to deserve a slide of its own, the slide should stay up long enough to allow the audience to digest it thoroughly.

**Templates**

Earlier (pp. 3-4), we defined templates and explained their importance to the integrated look and feel of slide show. Here we'll spend some time understanding how templates can help you do your work more effectively.

Pre-defined styles. Every major PG package ships with several presentation templates (some have dozens) each of which imposes a unified graphic design over a set of slide types. If you need to create a title for your presentation, you will find a title slide. If you need bullet points, you'll find a bullet slide. If you need to design a graph, you'll find a slide that supports graph design, and so on.

These pre-defined designs can save you a lot of time. All of the little questions about where to place bullets, how to arrange text on a page, and what colors to choose have been established for you. Most PG software ships with a sufficiently diverse array of template options to satisfy a wide variety of audiences, topics, and situations.

However, as noted earlier, some templates are inappropriate for some topics, so you have to choose carefully. You do not want to strike a light note when broaching human tragedy, or use school-based metaphors in corporate training. Choose a template that is consistent with the goals you entertain for the speech itself.

A more subtle, but equally serious problem, is using a template that has the potential of interfering with the text and/or images you present. Such interference comes in two forms: crowding out text, and presenting screen elements that confuse the substance of the presentation. Of the two, the crowding problem is easier to identify. Some template frames are very heavy, taking up a large percentage of screen real estate for repetitive, non-substantive elements. Avoid these designs unless you have a very good reason for using the repetitive graphic elements they depict.

More dangerous than that is the template that imposes random design features over information, making it easy to mistake one for the other. Consider the following slide on Web use:

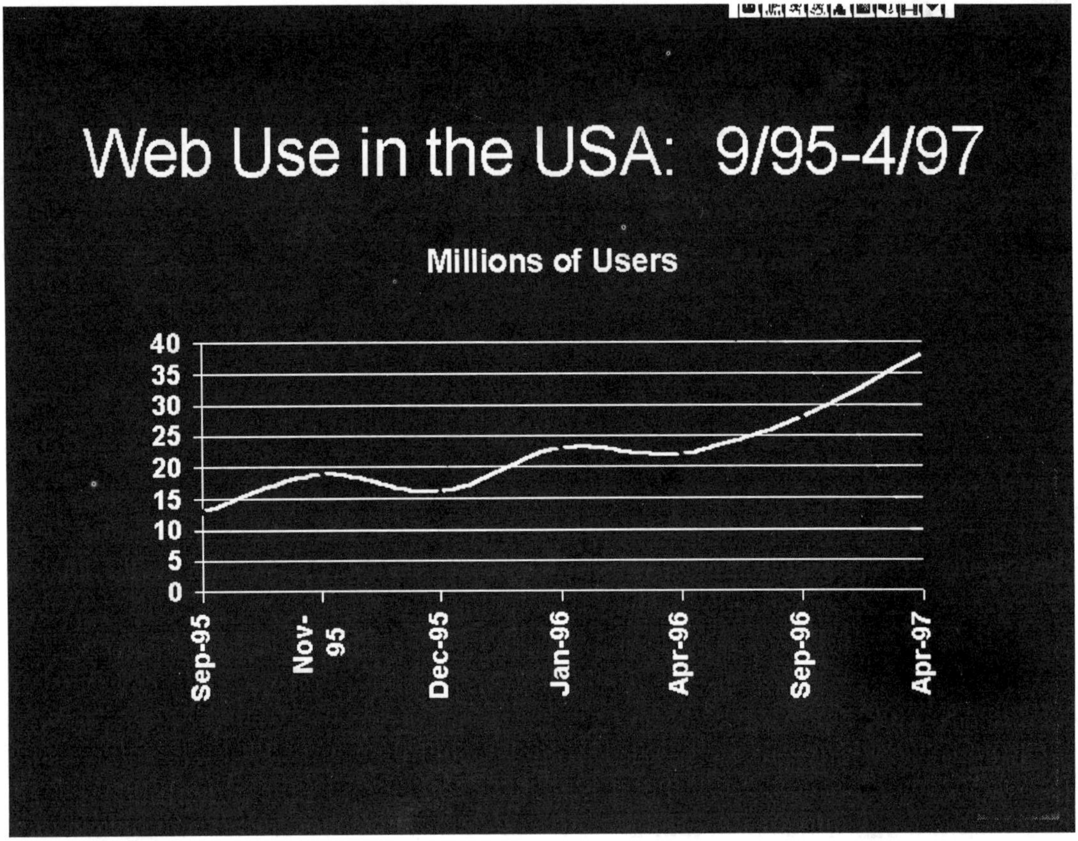


Here the line graph is challenged by another line resident on the template. The curving figure that enters the plane of the graph shortly before "Sep-96" makes the information harder to see. Worse, some viewers could interpret this line as a another data point, indicating a drop-off in Web use while there was actually a large increase during the period represented on the *X*-axis. This is a small problem in color, but a serious problem in black and white. The template in question, "Soaring.pot" from Microsoft PowerPoint™, prints only the swooping edge of the colored delta in black and white mode, aggravating the tension between design and data.

The template used elsewhere in this presentation, "Sidebar.pot," also from PowerPoint™, does not include design elements that conflict with data. It is a plain design, but effective, particularly for conservative audiences or serious topics. You may well want to use a more active template, but remember that the activity may step on your message, your data, or both. Choose carefully and make sure that your tools match your mission.

Template masters. Though templates pre-package many of the design decisions you have to make yourself, you do have the option to retain the benefits of templating while customizing the designs to your own purposes. You could do that by modifying screen elements one by one on each page, but that takes unnecessary time. Far more efficient is the practice of modifying the template itself.

You can do just that by invoking the template master command in your software. Programs vary in the degree of flexibility they offer you in modifying basic template designs, but most will allow you to shift the placement of recurrent elements (such as the line under the title in Sidebar.pot), the default font sizes at various levels, colors, and other features. Remember that when you make a change in the template master, you make a change in every slide in the show. Use this function if you want a global change of that magnitude, not to move one text box a little up and to the left on a single slide.

**The Slide Window**

All of your design will take place in the slide window of your presentation software. This is where you do the basic work of entering text and data, choosing slide formats, adjusting fonts, and adding presentation effects. You will find the slide window surrounded with icons that invoke various tools for inserting text, for drawing, and for a host of other functions.

Don't be intimidated. It looks like a lot, but you don't need to use everything all at once. In fact, you probably shouldn't try. Get acquainted with the basic functions of the program before exploiting the more advanced resources. For most presentations, the basic functions are the ones you'll want in any case. Remember, these programs are intended to speed the design process for people who are not professional designers; take advantage! Use what comes most easily and then build into new features as you find that you need them.

You can do most of what you need to do simply by clicking on an entry field, and then filling in whatever it is you want your audience to see. The following screen is from PowerPoint'sTM slide view. Certain features are unique to PowerPointTM, but the general practice of pointing an clicking is very much the same in other PG packages.

As you can see, there are spaces in which you can type your title, your major headings, subpoints, and anything else you think necessary on the slide.

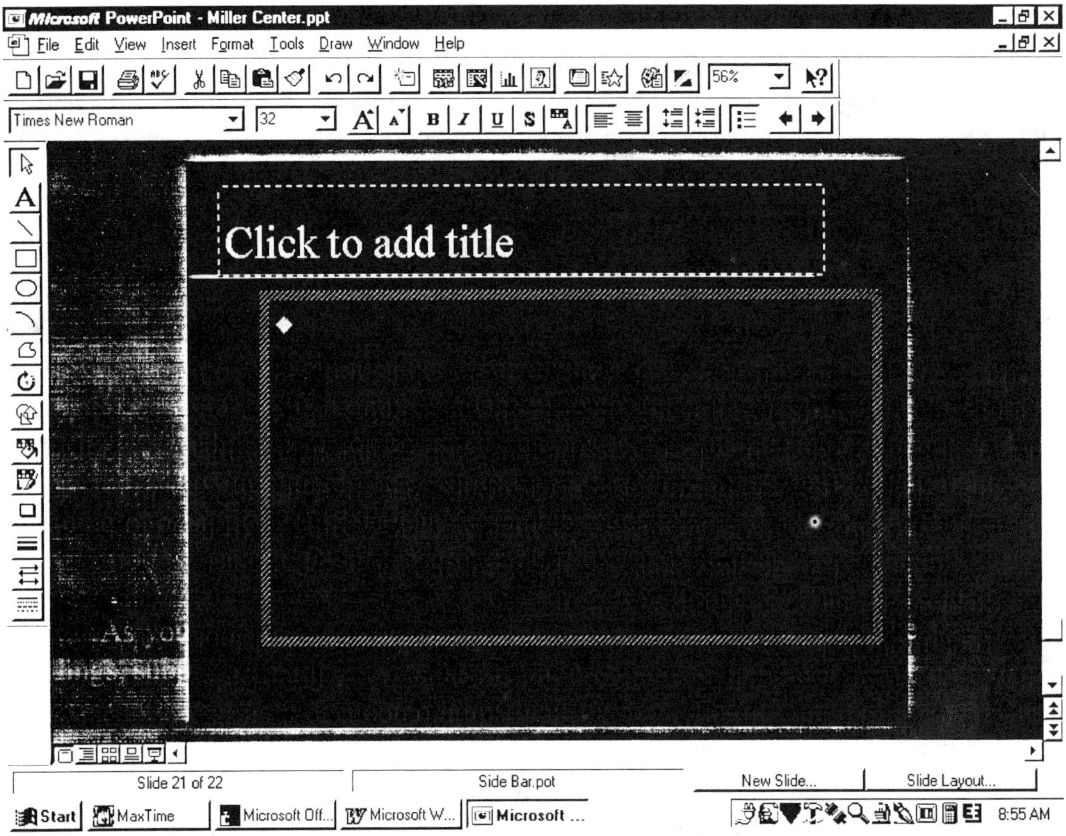


The button bars across the top, bottom, and sides provide tools to customize text, navigate the screen or the entire slide show, insert new slides, and play back whatever has been done to allow the author to see what it all looks like. There's no need to remember arcane commands for these simple operations; everything you need to produce a basic text slide is a mouse click away.

Because features and interfaces vary from program to program, we won't go beyond this very basic overview here. The important point to remember is that the program guides you along the way. In this sense, the PG program can be even easier than learning a word processing package, where you're presented with a strip of icons, a white page, and a blinking cursor. In PowerPoint™ and in other programs, you are told where to click and what the template asks you to insert there. You'll still be responsible for the content, but the program helps you to put it in the right places.

**Tips for Text Slides**

The purposes of a text slide are simple. You want to help your audience recognize and follow your structure, underline the important points that you want them to remember, and provide a useful speaking outline for yourself. Your PG package will provide you with tools to do all of that.

A key point in constructing text slides is to remember that the slides should support your oral presentation, not substitute for it. Never show the audience a slide that you do not plan to discuss in some detail. The text gives you a way to help identify and clarify ideas for the audience; if you use the tool to introduce ideas different from the ones you're speaking about, the result will be confusion. Attention – the most precious commodity an audience has to offer – will be diffused over two parallel sequences of information rather than focused tightly on one. Use text slides to focus your agenda, not to broaden it. With that in mind, let's move on to specifics.

Keep it short. Showing an audience text during a speech is different from giving someone something to read. Reading is a solitary experience, best conducted in silence. If you give your audience a lengthy, text-heavy slide, you will encourage them to stop listening and start reading, rarely a desirable outcome for a speaker. Use short, declarative sentences or phrases for your bullet points. Avoid paragraphs. If you have a complex idea that you want to put up on the screen, try to break it up into bullets.

Fonts. Font controls determine the size of the type that appears in various areas of the slide. It would be nice if there were a rule of thumb about font sizes, but differences in display make that unrealistic. A 16-point font may look fine if it's projected from an overhead onto a large screen, but that same 16-point font will look much smaller when displayed on a 27-inch monitor.

You can safely assume that you'll have to use sizes of at least 16 points to be seen on any display medium, and some elements, such as titles, will have to be much larger than that, perhaps between 44 and 54 points. The defaults in your PG package will get you into the ballpark, but remember, you're not in a ballpark. You'll be speaking in a specific room with specific display equipment. You may find that you'll have to increase all font sizes to make text visible at the back of the room.

Builds. Build functions allow you to reveal your slide progressively. This is one of the handiest tools available to you when presenting directly from a computer. By hiding speech elements before you get to them, you prevent your audience's attention from drifting ahead of your oral delivery.

If you choose to use builds, use them consistently. Having some slides built and other static lend a haphazard quality to the presentation. Likewise, if you use a dimming or graying control to change the appearance of bullets that you've already covered, make sure that you use it consistently throughout the presentation. Don't design in so many builds that the audience is constantly assaulted with new information that disappears just as quickly as it arrives.

Level of detail. Most PG software supports multiple levels of indentation, but you'll probably want to use only the first two, and perhaps, on occasion, the third. Font balance – fonts get smaller with indentation – means that indents get hard to see very quickly. They can clutter a screen and present an overly complicated visual "aid" for your audience. Sticking to the first- and second-level builds can solve this problem.

**Tips for Graphic Slides**

Graphic slides can be some of the most powerful devices you can use, but you need to use them cautiously. It is not a good idea to include graphics willy-nilly just because the computer gives you that option. Instead, choose graphics that show relationships, illustrate unique persons, places, or things, and clarify abstract or data-heavy concepts.

Graphs. A great deal has been written on graph design; we can only mention a couple of points here. Consult the references at the end of this booklet for further information on the uses and abuses of graphs. Like your other design work, graph design takes place in the slide window. Typically, your PG software will have a slide format specifically for graphs. To construct the graph, you double click in a graph area, and a "datasheet" – a table that provides values for the graph output – pops up, into which you can then begin to insert your figures.

You can make this process much easier by cutting and pasting information from a spreadsheet or other data analysis software. That way you can use the fully-featured tools of a spreadsheet or a statistical package to analyze your data, then import the results into your presentation. This is not necessary, however; the data can be entered directly into the datasheet.

Check your graph's colors on your display equipment. The wide variety of colors used on graphs to identify different data elements makes it imperative that your display can adequately differentiate screen elements. All major presentation packages allow you to change the colors of bars or lines displaying data. A sequence of data is generally referred to as a "series;" check in your reference manual under that term or "data series" to find out how fully you can manipulate output.

Finally, do not fall into the trap of assuming that the flashiest graph is always the best. Three dimensional graphs can look great, but they can also be confusing, hiding lesser values behind greater, and making it difficult to see how a near column relates to a distant. Often, you'll be better off with plain-old 2-D graphics. Experiment! Switching from 2-D to 3-D views as well as switching from bar to line (and other) chart types is only a mouse click away.

Images. Most PG packages will accept a variety of images. Many ship with a good deal of clip art, typically including a variety of simple line drawings, symbols, and background elements. Third-party vendors sell more sophisticated clip art, and of course, you can always draw or scan your own images.

Be careful when scanning images or using images that you've obtained elsewhere. If you didn't do the photography or the drawing yourself, you could be making inappropriate use of copyrighted material. Always check with the owner of the image (which is *not* always the artist) to see if you have permission to use it in your presentation. This is particularly critical if you are presenting in a commercial context rather than a classroom.

The key consideration in using images is relevance. Many concepts, particularly concepts relating to spatial arrangement, are best illustrated with a graphic of some kind. Photographs and still frames from videos or movies are often the best way to get an audience to understand the differences between two apparently similar items. For these purposes, graphics are a godsend. Decoration, however, is a poor reason for inserting an image. If you can't come up with a reason stronger than "it looks nice," don't use it.

Clip art can be very useful in providing you with elements of your own drawings. The architectural and interior design elements of some clip art packages make room layouts extremely easy for even inexperienced users. But be careful. Clip art is by its nature generic, and because it is bundled with major software packages, everyone has access to it. Your presentation will not look unique if you are using the same clip art that three speakers ahead of you and two behind were using.

Remember that images often take up a lot of space on your hard drive. Be careful! Putting several graphics into a presentation can make it too big to fit on a floppy diskette. If your presentation equipment is networked so that you can transfer files without resorting to a diskette, file size may not be a problem. Alternatively, if you have access to large format removable storage, such as Iomega's Zip™ drive, *and that same large-format device can be attached to the presentation machine*, you can cart about files that are dozens of megabytes in size. For those presenters who must carry their materials about on a floppy, however, make sure that your presentation actually fits on the diskette.

Cutting down on the number of colors and the image resolution will make the graphic files you use smaller than they would be otherwise, but there is a cost in image quality. Two rules of thumb describe the boundaries: 1) don't reduce image quality past what you need to make your point, and 2) don't bother with image quality that exceeds the capabilities of your output device. If you're giving a presentation on open heart surgery and the audience absolutely must see the suture pattern on an arterial resect, then don't use a low-resolution graphic. The grainy image wouldn't provide you with the detail you need. If, on the other hand, you'll be using a display that produces only 256 colors, it's silly to cart around images with 16.7 million colors; the last 16,699,744 colors are just wasted file space because no one can see them.

## Basic Processes: Presentation

No matter how experienced a speaker you are, you'll need to invest some time learning how to use your presentation package in front of an audience. PG software gives you an enormous range of tools, but it also requires new disciplines. Machines are also notoriously peculiar and persnickety, so it's essential to become familiar with the equipment you'll be using yourself. Our discussion here will focus on presenting with a computer rather than printing out to overheads and presenting from acetates placed on a slide projector.

**Placing Your Equipment**

Equipment can help a speaker convey a point, or it can literally come between the presenter and the audience. You'll better ensure that your presentations fit into the former category by keeping your back to the screen. Many presenters make the mistake of watching their own slide shows. This socks them with the double whammy of losing eye contact with the audience and placing the slideshow at the center of attention. You can avoid both problems by keeping your back to the screen. When you need to refer to screen elements, you can step to the side of the screen, or turn briefly to check whatever it is you need to see. If you can position a computer monitor so that it faces you (in addition to the larger screen facing the audience), so much the better. You can see everything that happens on screen without ever having to turn around.

People with considerable experience using presentation graphics may be able to cue their own notes off of the screen rather than keeping a separate set of notes for themselves. Most of us, however, benefit from having a set of speaker's notes with us at the podium. Not only will this provide more detail than the text slides on the screen, it will also better ensure that you keep your eyes away from your slideshow.

**Use a Large, Legible Screen**

Everyone in the room has to be able to see the screen. In all but the smallest rooms, that means finding a large screen. If you use a projection technology such as an LCD or three-beam projector, or a flat-panel display mounted on an overhead projector, you'll be able to display large images, limited only by the size of the projection surface and the ambient light in the room. As a rule of thumb, a projected display gets dimmer as the source of the light moves further back, so in general, the larger the image size, the dimmer the picture.

You may well have to reduce the ambient lighting in the room, easy enough in windowless spaces, but sometimes difficult in rooms with lot of natural light. Sometimes it's worth sacrificing size for brightness; at other times, the reverse is true. Test different configurations and see what works best.

If you have the proper equipment, you might also choose to use a large monitor to display your slideshow. The bright display of the monitor makes it useful for cases in which you want to retain overhead lighting, and it is particularly effective for smaller meetings. For any presentation to more than a half-dozen people, however, you will need a monitor of at least 35 inches. Again, the secret is experimentation. Put up the slide with the greatest detail and move around the room to ensure that everyone can see what you've prepared.

Don't make the mistake of standing in front of the screen or monitor, a problem that gets harder to avoid in shallower, wider rooms. If there is no way to avoid obscuring someone's view, make sure that you move around enough to allow everyone a look at every slide. Leaving audience members without a line of sight is as good as saying that you don't care about their opinions!

**Input Devices**

One of the great benefits of a computerized presentation is the progressive revelation of content across and within slides. But that progress cannot take place without some way of conveying commands to the computer. Most presentation packages advance screen elements one at a time on mouse clicks, pressing the space bar, pressing a cursor arrow, or all three. If you do use the mouse or the keyboard, remember that you will be, in essence, tethered to the computer. Make sure that the computer is placed comfortably so that you don't have to cross the screen every time you want to advance a slide.

Several companies market infrared or radio-controlled devices that give you mouse functions from a distance. These are very useful tools for presenters, particularly in large rooms. Like any other tool, however, they take some practice. Don't begrudge yourself the time in testing new equipment before the presentation begins.

**Handouts**

PG software makes it very easy to construct handouts with the content of your slides. Such handouts are extremely useful for guiding audience note-taking. Rather than trying to get down every detail, members of the audience can focus on the larger concepts in the presentation.

Speakers differ on their preferences for distributing handouts before or after a presentation. Prior distribution makes clear to the audience what they do and do not have to copy down during the talk. Post-speech distribution can focus greater attention on the speaker, as there is always a risk that audience members will simply stop listening in order to read ahead in the handout. Mid-speech distribution gives you the worst of both worlds. Passing around materials disrupts the flow of the presentation. Audience members, having already settled into a note taking routine, will have that routine interrupted, further distracting from the speech. And finally, anyone who wants to can read ahead from the point of distribution on.

In general, for information-rich presentations, you're probably better off with a pre-speech distribution. That way everyone can gauge a pattern of response to the speech and orient themselves to a particular variety of note taking behavior. When in doubt, make your audience more comfortable, not less.

## Pitfalls

These pitfalls are the seven deadly sins of using presentation graphics. Take heed here, and don't let any of this happen to you.

1. **Cutesy Graphics.** Many presentations are rife with pointless clip art, balloons, fireworks, holiday wreaths, and other pointless addenda. Not only do these elements clutter presentations, they raise the very real prospect of including images that the audience will associate with a very different meaning. Consider the case of a presenter speaking on behalf of a hospital who uses the caduceus (the snake and staff emblem). If the speaker follows someone who had just condemned the medical establishment with reference to the "snake," each appearance of the piece of clip art will remind the audience of the indictment, detracting from the force of the presentation.

2. **Animations.** Most presentation graphics packages allow you to fully animate the slideshow. In other words, the screen and bullets would advance without any speaker input; working instead from a timer set during slideshow construction. Be very careful of animations of this sort! They can easily get away from the speaker and begin popping up new information before the old information has been covered. Even under the best of circumstances, these features require split second timing from the speaker – very difficult to achieve in unscripted speeches. There are very few good reasons to animate slideshows. Animations within a slide you control yourself are fine, just don't loose control of the sequence of the presentation

3. **Tiny Type.** Everyone knows they need to check font sizes; nonetheless, people consistently put tiny, illegible type in front of audiences. Few things alienate an

audience so quickly as having to strain to see a screen. Make sure that you don't put your listeners through this ordeal.

4. **Too Many Slides.** Some presenters try to cram too many slides into a speech. This results in one of two problems. Either they go overtime, or they pull slides off the screen faster than the audience can see them. Either result can provoke considerable frustration from the audience. Plan on spending at least a minute with every slide you use. If it doesn't justify the investment of sixty seconds, it probably isn't work showing in the first place.

5. **Overly Complex Slides.** This is the flip side of having too many slides. Some presenters feel it necessary to cram a lot of information onto a very few slides, making it hard for the audience to follow the train of thought and encouraging font-squeezing. Try to keep large ideas separate from one another on different slides. Make sure that you've allocated enough space to have the points stand out clearly from one another.

6. **Failure to Check the Room.** The best planning in the world cannot improve a slideshow that won't work in the presentation space. Make sure that you check your room and your equipment. Trusting to luck will certainly cause you grief sooner or later.

7. **Allowing the Screen to Become the Focus of the Presentation.** We've talked about this before, but it bears repeating: you should be the center of attention not your slideshow. If the audience is paying more attention to the screen than to you, you might as well just send them a video with the slideshow.

## Other Sources

For additional information on graph design, you will find a wealth of detail in three books by Edward Tufte. *The Visual Display of Quantitative Information* (Graphics Press, 1983), is the one most closely tied to graphing per se. *Envisioning Information* (Graphics Press, 1991), and *Visual Explanations* (Graphics Press, 1997) are broader treatments of graphic design (still with an emphasis on representing data. All three books are theoretically rich, beautifully illustrated, and packed with examples drawn from all over the world. Stephen Kosslyn's *Elements of Graph*

*Design* (Freeman, 1994) offers a different take on similar material. Kosslyn is a cognitive psychologist with a good deal to say about basic principles in graph design. His book is organized as a practical guide, so if you're in a hurry, this is a good place to go.

There are any number of good books available on basic principles of typography, page layout, and other professional graphic design issues. A good introduction is Robin Williams, *The Non-Designer's Design Book* (Peachpit Press, 1994).

And there is, of course, a multitude of titles dealing with individual software programs. Like the software itself, the books change constantly. Look for reviews in *PC Magazine*, *MacWorld*, and other computer periodicals. If you can't find computer books at your campus bookstore, you can always use the World Wide Web to browse offerings at the Computer Literacy Bookstores and other online retailers.

## A Quick Guide to Preparing Presentation Graphics

**Sample Presentation: Inequalities on the Internet**

Before you even begin to think about using your graphics package, you'll want to have a clear idea of who your audience will be and what the topic is. Develop a focused thesis statement from the general topic area, and make sure that you have the information you need to defend that thesis.

***Prepare your speech outline.*** Put the substance of your speech into a topical outline. At this stage, the outline can be lean, detailed, or somewhere in the middle; you'll probably be modifying the outline as you work your way through the PG package and decide what issues to emphasize. What are the main points you're trying to raise? Will the audience understand these issues easily, or will they need a good deal of contextual information to make sense of what you're saying?

***Decide which points your graphics should address.*** Is your argument predicated on figures? If so, what kind of graph will do the best job of representing those figures? Remember that while numbers are often powerful tools for exposition and persuasion, they can also quickly over-saturate an audience. Identify the numbers most crucial to your case; don't include less relevant numbers simply because you have them available.

In our hypothetical case, we have survey data indicating that Internet use in the United States is distributed unevenly by age, gender, region, income, and urbanicity. The data are themselves crucial to our argument. We have to make the audience understand some characteristics of the general population as well as the specified characteristics of the Internet user population. Our most important goal will be to convince the audience of the disparities and gain consensus for focused attention to the problem.

**Stepping through the Design**

***Pick a template.*** This is a serious, public policy issue that will demand close attention from our audience. We don't want to suggest, through the choice of festive graphics, that this subject can be treated lightly. We might also run into some problems with basic understanding from audience members who don't themselves use Internet technologies. For that reason, it's probably a bad idea to choose a "techie" look. A plain, uncluttered background would probably be best. We'll take Side Bar.pot, the same PowerPoint™ template you saw earlier in the booklet.

***Choose a title.*** Choosing the title slide is easy. Every template comes with one; all you need to do is click on the appropriate design and click "OK". Choosing the title is somewhat harder. The title should correspond closely to the thesis statement (in this case: we must ensure that the benefits of the Internet are equally available to all citizens). We might also consider using the combination of a title and a subtitle to make the issue clear from the outset. Here, we might choose something like the one below. This title slide doesn't push the thesis too early, but it plainly introduces the themes that makes the thesis work. The words on the screen reinforce the sense of the presentation: access is a social justice issue.

***Incorporate the outline into the slideshow.*** Here you need to take the major categories in the presentation and put them onto slides. Start with your preview, a brief roadmap telling the audience where you're going in the presentation. Preview slides should contain reference only to major categories.

Remember that while the slides can serve as your notes, that's a secondary role for screen content. You may need more detail than you want to give the audience. Use the speaker's notes screen to accomplish that task; don't burden the screen text with more verbiage than it can bear.

***Pose your major argument(s).*** A key element of this case is proof that there is indeed differential use of the Internet, a claim we base on survey data. Early in the presentation, we'll want to present those data. There are too many issues to try to deal with on a single slide. We'll have to make our case over several slides.

In the following example, usage of the Internet by age, a side-by-side bar chart shows our results most effectively. The side-by-side elements make it easy to see an age group's representation in the general population, and then their representation in four classes of computer use.

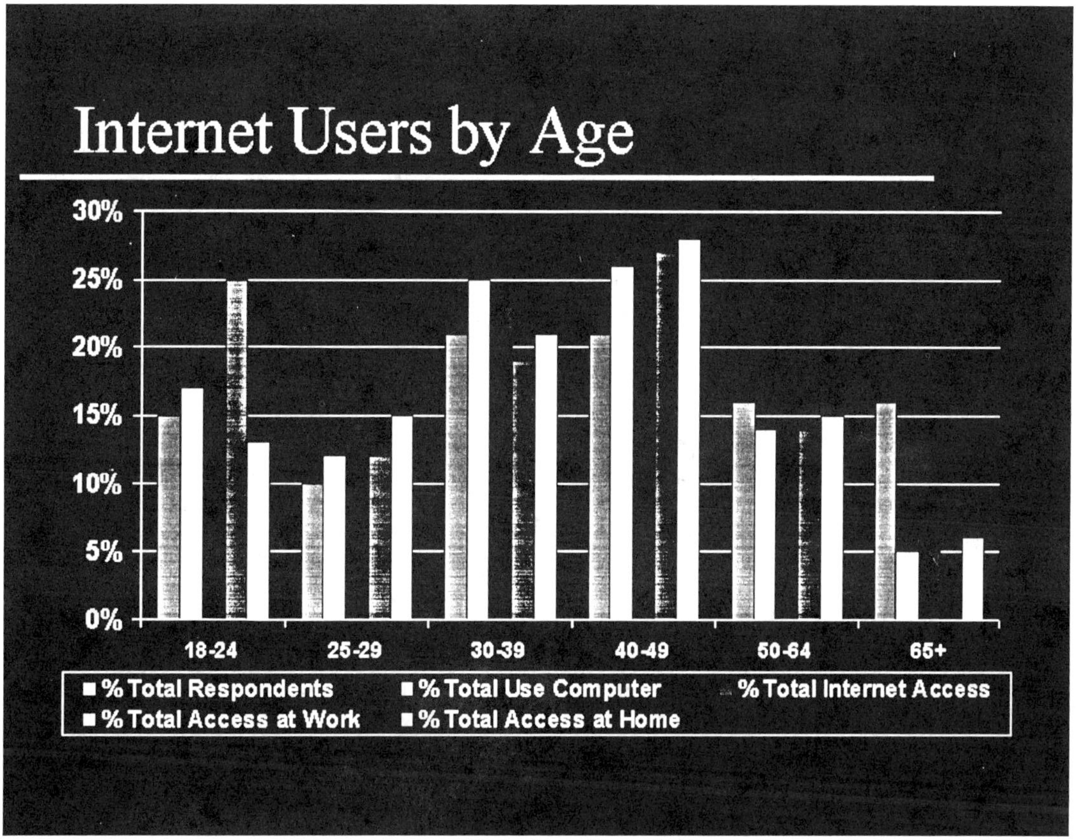


Data from Baruch-Harris Survey Unit, April 1997

We could construct similar charts to show discrepancies by the other factors we have identified: gender, region, income, and urbanicity. If there are relatively few datapoints, it might be possible to combine descriptors on the same chart. Take a look at page four for a combined view of the region and urbanicity data.

***Prune your text slides.*** In the following example, the first screen is too wordy. The second screen takes similar concepts but presents them in a form much better suited to visual presentations.

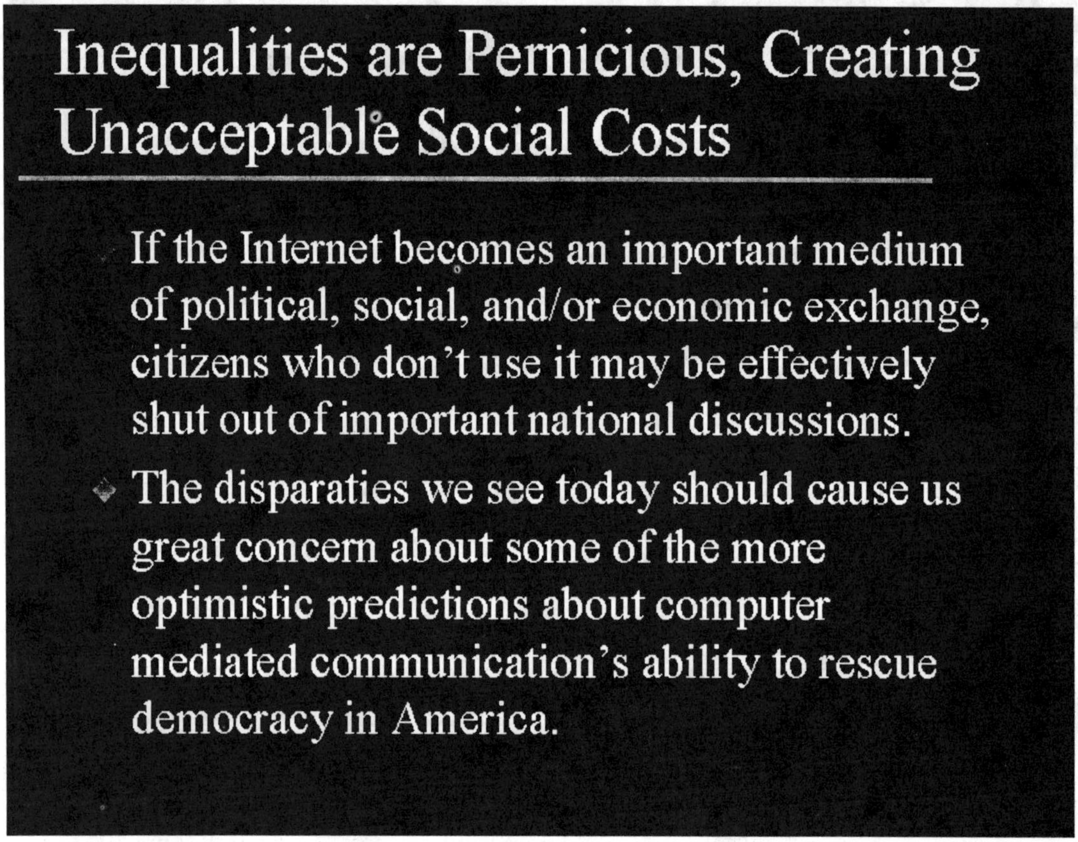


Not only is this screen wordy, it also offers a poor match between the title and the slide text. Note that there isn't anything particularly wrong with the bulleted sentences; they might work well on the printed page. They are, however, too long to serve a speaker as a bridge to an audience. The following example makes better use of the graphic conventions that viewers expect from a presentation program.

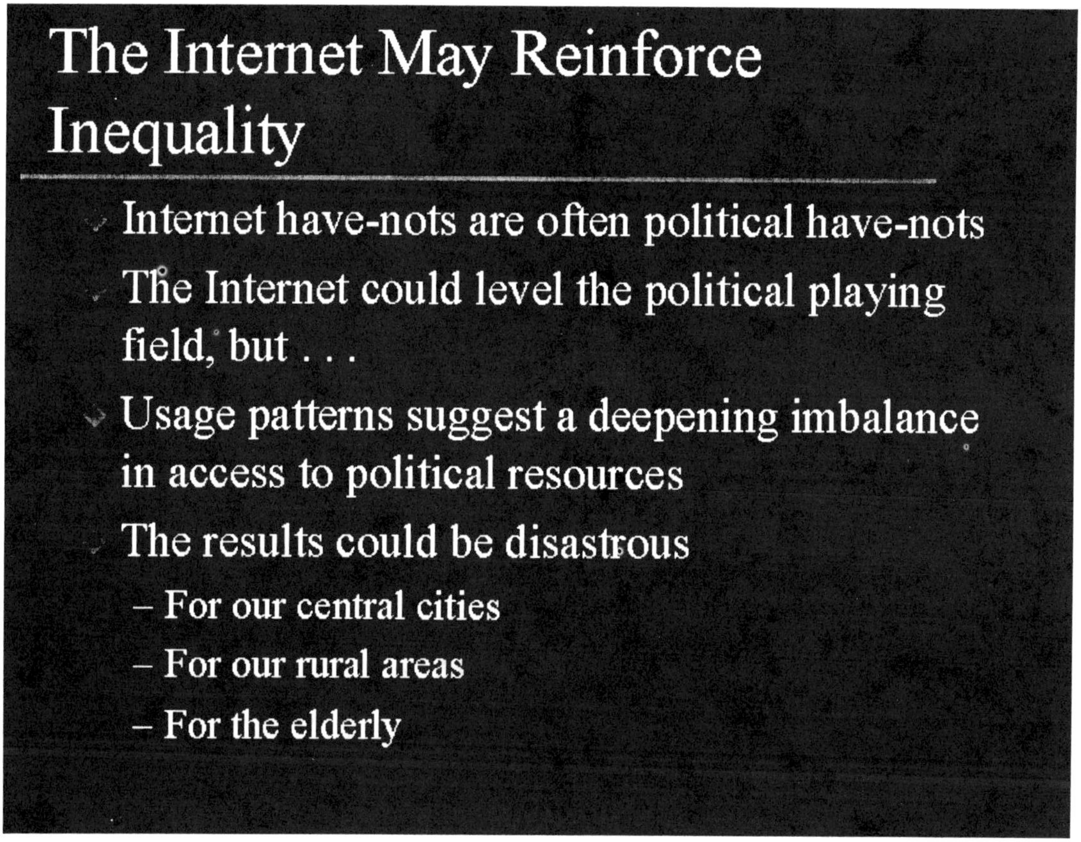


Unlike the first slide, this slide provides smaller units of text that will be easier to build onscreen. The logic of the builds also lends some drama to the presentation. Instead of asking the audience to digest large chunks of text, it presents small units that prompt fuller discussion from you, the speaker.

Continue to prepare your text slides in this way, pruning unnecessary verbiage to meet the demands of computer-driven presentation. It is critical that you remain flexible. Many presentations have suffered from early commitment to a structure that later proves to be inappropriate. Don't lock yourself in now; work back and forth between your own understanding of the outline and what you think makes the best sense for consumption onscreen.

***Review your work.*** Don't stop with the last slide; go right back to the beginning and check your work. Do the slides flow smoothly, one to the other? Have you put in all of the builds you want? Ask a friend to look at the graphs; do they make sense without undue explanation. Remember, you never want to use a graph that hinders your presentation; they're supposed to make concepts easier. If that's not the case, try another type until you get it right.

***Practice the speech.*** Even if you're an accomplished speaker, you'll want some practice with your speech. That is particularly important if you're new to presentation graphics. Getting your rhythm down can be a little tricky at first if you haven't had experience moving back to the mouse or keyboard to advance a slide. It will come easily enough, but don't expect it to happen smoothly if your first experience is in front of the "real" audience.

***Check your room and equipment.*** Assume that what can go wrong, will go wrong. You'll need to ensure that you have either the correct presentation package on the screen or a usable run-time program (a portable module that allows you to execute a slideshow without loading the whole program on the presentation computer). Check the ambient lighting in the room; can you see the smallest elements on all of your screens? Are the fonts large enough for the people in the back row? Checking now will prevent grief later.

Now you're ready to present!